Baby's First ABCs Book

Select a letter, color the picture, and let the baby's learning begin!

Date: ....

Time: ....

Location: ....

....

....

Tape Your
Photo Here

PICTURE OF ME

A

is for

Apple

With love, _____

B

is for

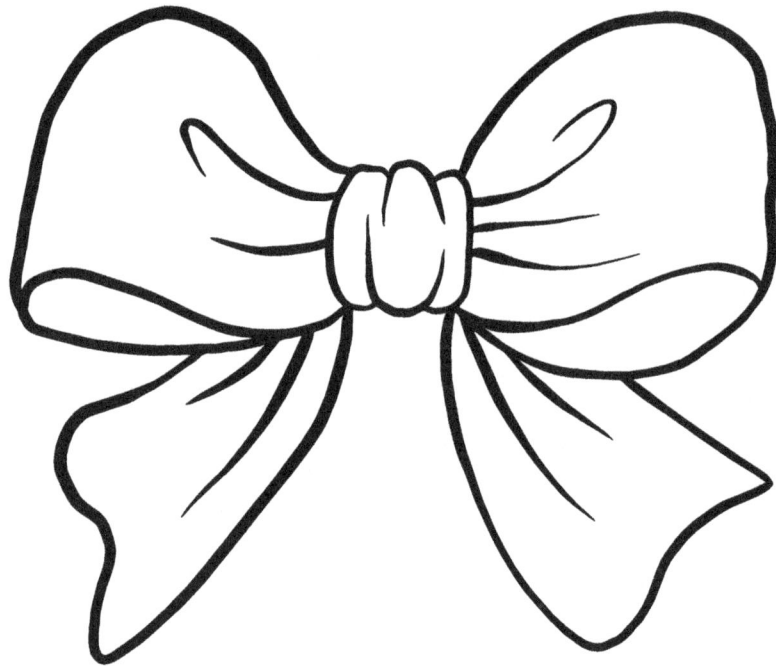

Bow

With love, _____

C

C is for

Cat

With love, _____

D is for

Dog

With love, _____

E

is for

Elephant

With love, _____

F

is for

Frog

With love, _____

G is for

Gifts

With love, _____

H is for

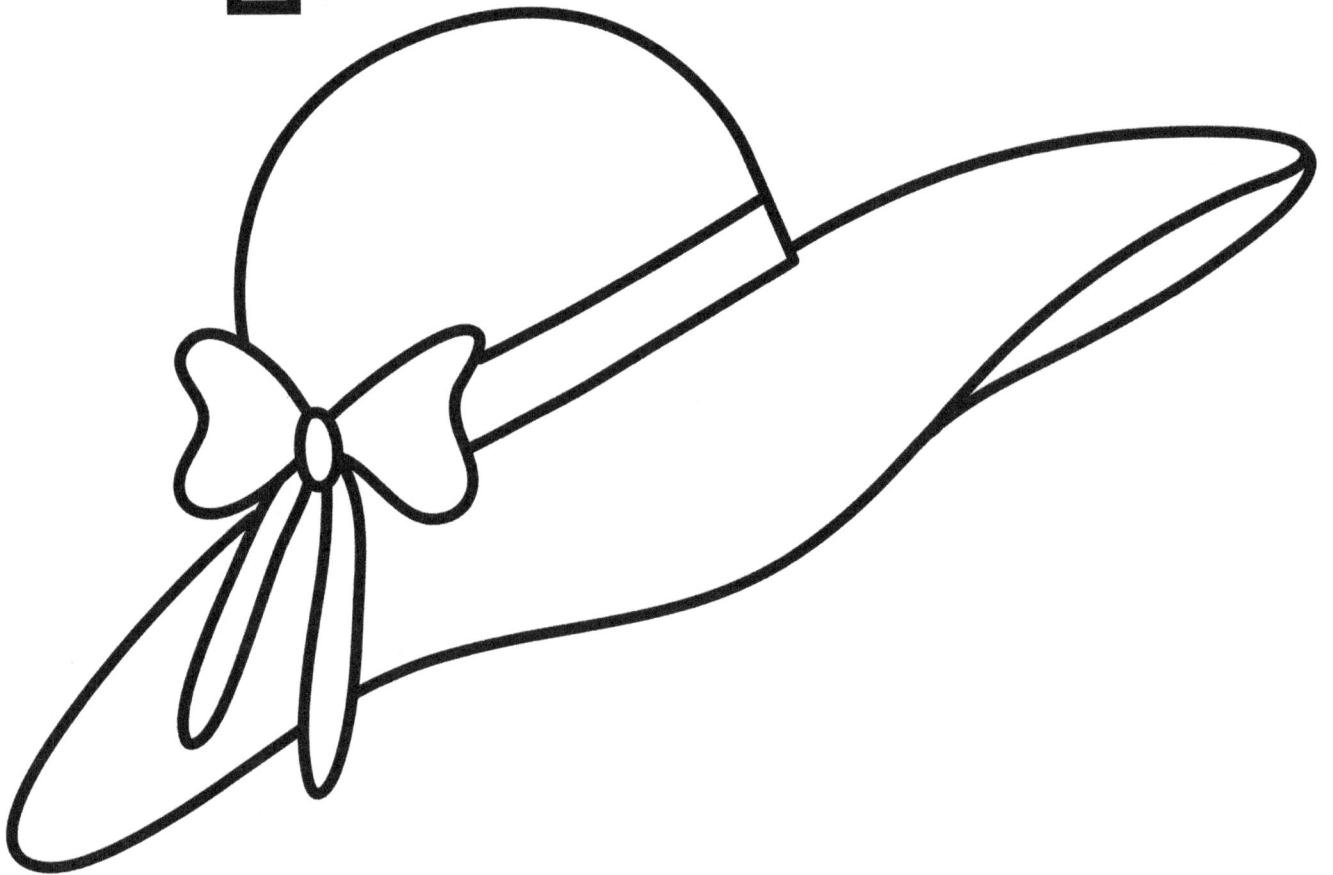

Hat

With love, _____

I is for

Ice Cream

With love, _____

J is for

Jacket

With love, _____

K is for

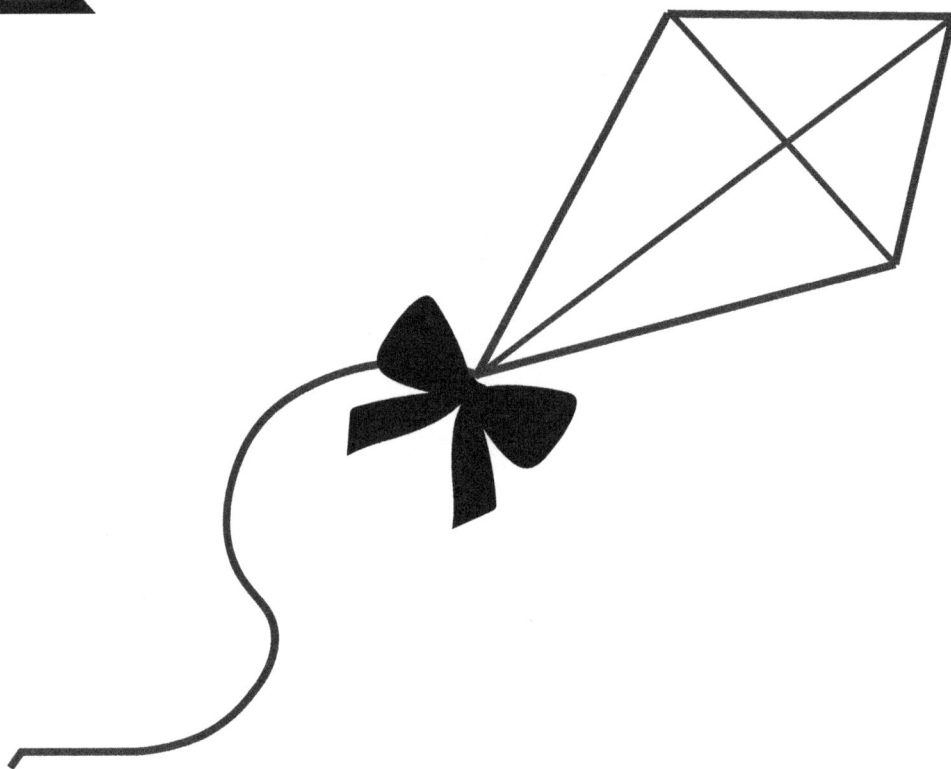

Kite

With love,_____

L

is for

Ladybug

With love, _____

M is for

Monkey

With love, _____

N is for

Newborn

With love, _____

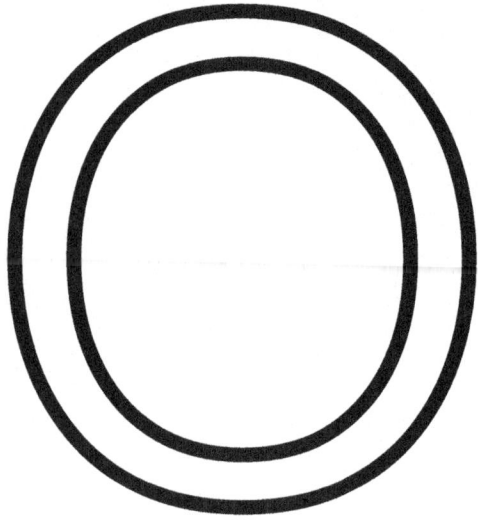 is for

Octopus

With love, _____

P is for

Parrot

With love, _____

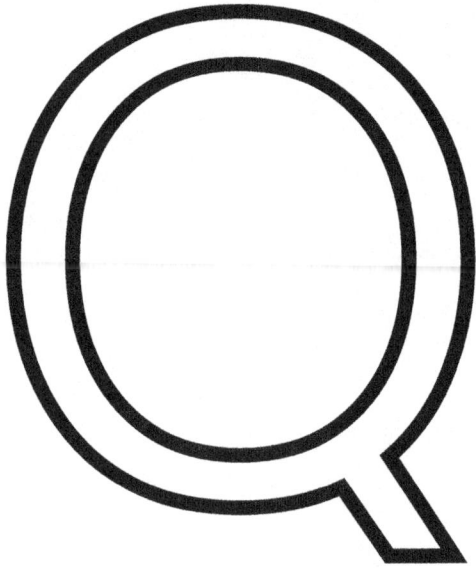 **is for**

Quilt

With love, _____

R

is for

Rabbit

With love, _____

S is for

Sock

With love, _____

T is for

Turtle

With love, _____

U is for

Umbrella

With love, _____

V is for

Violin

With love, _____

W

is for

Whale

With love,_____

X is for

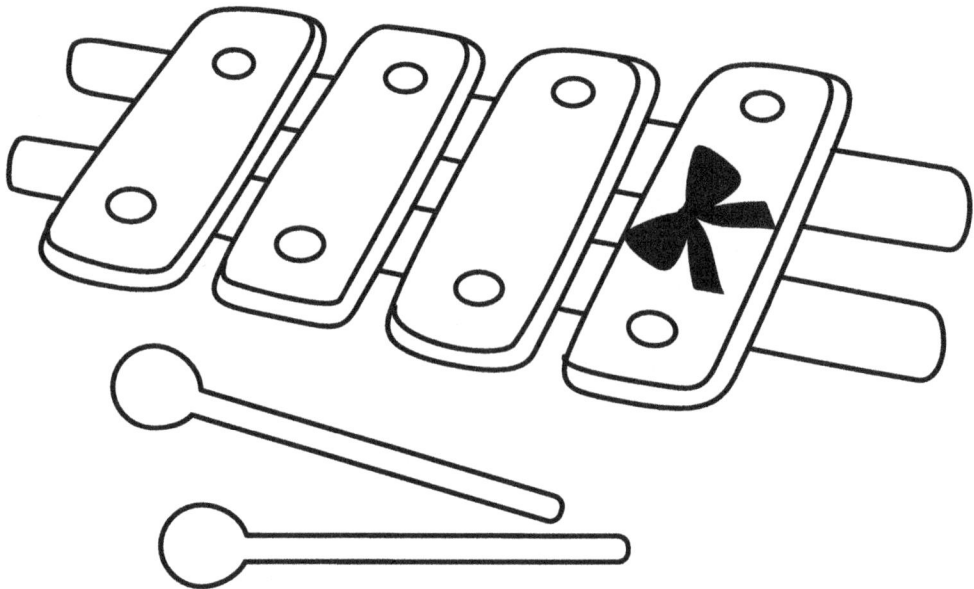

Xylophone

With love, _____

Y

is for

Yarn

With love, _____

Z is for

Zebra

With love, _____

Tape Your
Photo Here

Tape Your
Photo Here

Tape Your
Photo Here

Tape Your
Photo Here

Tape Your
Photo Here

Tape Your
Photo Here

Tape Your
Photo Here

GIFTS RECEIVED

Name _____

Gift Given _____

Name _____

Gift Given _____

Name _____

Gift Given _____

Name _____

Gift Given _____

Name _____

Gift Given _____

Name _____

Gift Given _____

Name _____

Gift Given _____

Name _____

Gift Given _____

Name _____

Gift Given _____

Name _____

Gift Given _____

Name _____

Gift Given _____

Name _____

Gift Given _____

Name _____

Gift Given _____

Name _____

Gift Given _____

Name _____

Gift Given _____

Name _____

Gift Given _____

Name _____

Gift Given _____

Name _____

Gift Given _____

Name _____

Gift Given _____

Name _____

Gift Given _____

Name _____

Gift Given _____

Name _____

Gift Given _____

Name _____

Gift Given _____

Name _____

Gift Given _____

Name _____

Gift Given _____

Name _____

Gift Given _____

Name _____

Gift Given _____

Name _____

Gift Given _____

Name _____

Gift Given _____

Name _____

Gift Given _____

Name _____

Gift Given _____

Name _____

Gift Given _____

Name _____

Gift Given _____

Name _____

Gift Given _____

Name _____

Gift Given _____

Name _____

Gift Given _____

Name _____

Gift Given _____

Name _____

Gift Given _____

Name _____

Gift Given _____

Name _____

Gift Given _____

Name _____

Gift Given _____

Name _____

Gift Given _____

Name _____

Gift Given _____

Name _____

Gift Given _____

Name _____

Gift Given _____

Name _____

Gift Given _____

Name _____

Gift Given _____

Name _____

Gift Given _____

Name _____

Gift Given _____

MEMORIES

MEMORIES

MEMORIES

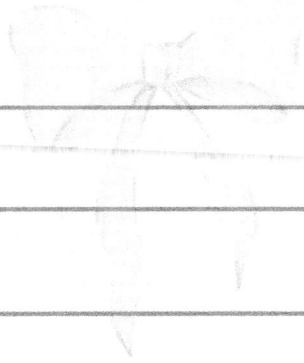

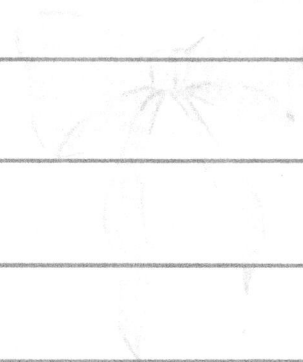

We would love to have your feedback.
Congratulations!

Scan

Me

Made in the USA
Coppell, TX
10 June 2025